Marvin Leynar

Dr. Gardner's book ought to be of immense help to boys & girls & parents in a divorce situation. Interesting & to the point.

THE BOYS AND GIRLS BOOK ABOUT DIVORCE

WITH AN INTRODUCTION FOR PARENTS

THE BOYS AND GIRLS BOOK ABOUT DIVORCE

WITH AN INTRODUCTION FOR PARENTS

by RICHARD A. GARDNER, M.D.

Associate in Child Psychiatry
College of Physicians and Surgeons   Columbia University

Faculty   William A. White Psychoanalytic Institute
New York, New York

Foreword by Louise Bates Ames, Ph.D.
Associate Director   Gesell Institute   New Haven, Conn.

ILLUSTRATED BY ALFRED LOWENHEIM

Library of Congress Catalog Card Number: 72-110254
Standard Book Number: 87668-032-5

BOOK DESIGNED BY RUTH BORNSCHLEGEL

Manufactured by Haddon Craftsmen, Inc.
Scranton, Pennsylvania

TO LEE, ANDY, NANCY, AND JULIE

ACKNOWLEDGMENTS

MOST OF WHAT I have recorded in this book about the reactions of children to divorce has been derived from my therapeutic work with such children. In a sense, much of the book was written by them, with the author serving as the collector and organizer of the information. Of the many children who have so contributed, I am particularly indebted to Anne, Barbara, John, Joni, Kathy, Kevin, Ronald, and Scott. Other children who deserve mention because of their assistance are Beth, Douglas, Jeffrey, Jonathan, Leo, Martin, Sara, and Stephanie. The interest, cooperation, and suggestions of the parents of these children are also deeply appreciated.

Of the friends and colleagues who were kind enough to read the text and offer suggestions, I am particularly grateful to Dr. Gerard Chrzanowski, Professor Frances Dubner, Mrs. Minna Genn, Dr. Clarice Kestenbaum, and Professor Michael Sovern.

Lastly, my most deep-felt gratitude goes to Lee, who as loving wife patiently tolerated the absences which the writing of this book necessitated and as respected colleague provided me with most meaningful and useful suggestions.

Richard A. Gardner M.D.

CONTENTS

FOREWORD

THOUGH IN MANY ways this is a troubled age, in other ways it's a rather wonderful time to be alive. It is a time when people's feelings are recognized, faced, respected, and handled with more consideration than ever before.

In the present volume, for example, for the first time, an author speaks directly and honestly to boys and girls about the feelings they may experience when their parents get divorced. He pulls no punches, but frankly faces the fact that for many it will be very hard going for a long while. Instead of glossing things over as many writers have tended to do in the past, he speaks clearly about some of the fears, anxieties, and sorrows such children will experience. He assures them they are not unique in having such feelings and that it is not wrong or unusual to feel as they do.

And then, for each problem he describes, he gives good practical advice as to things children can do to make themselves feel better and about things that will make life easier and more pleasant for them and for their parents.

Some of his ideas are entirely conventional. He supports many of the usual notions found in the literature on divorce: that most children are better off in a broken home than in an unhappy home; that parents must make every effort to avoid fighting their battles with each other through their children; that children of divorced parents must, if possible, avoid the temptation of trying to take the place of the missing parent; that children should, if possible, avoid using up a great deal of emotional energy in hoping, probably in vain, that their parents will remarry each other.

Less conventional are his contradictions of commonly held notions about what divorced parents should tell their children. For, example, he believes that if the absent parent clearly shows no interest whatever in the welfare of his children, the parent they live with should admit this unhappy fact to the child and help him come to terms with it. Hopefully, the child will come to realize that just because one parent does not love him, this does not mean that he is a bad person or not lovable.

He also gives the very realistic advice, again contrary to much in the previous literature on the subject, that each parent need not *always* say *only* good things about the other. Each should avoid bitterness and vituperation as much as possible, but each should also now and then truthfully admit that the other does have an occasional fault.

Both of these points are well taken, since obviously if a mother insists that the absent father loves his children in spite of all evidence to the contrary or if she pretends the absent father has no faults, her children are not going to believe or trust her.

This is by no means a Pollyanna sort of book. It faces many grave problems and sad, unhappy feelings frankly, but it is still cheerful and positive. For every problem raised it suggests either a solution or at least a practical, sensible way of facing a difficult and unhappy situation when it is inevitable.

There is no question in my mind that this book provides the most helpful information and guidance yet available for those young people—the children of divorced parents—who are faced with more trouble than many of them can handle. Such children will be infinitely less victimized by their situation if they follow even a portion of Dr. Gardner's excellent advice.

Louise Bates Ames, Ph.D.
Associate Director,
Gesell Institute

INTRODUCTION FOR PARENTS

MOST PSYCHIATRISTS agree that divorce *per se* does not necessarily cause psychiatric problems to develop in children. In fact, the child living with unhappily married parents more often gets into psychiatric difficulty than the one whose mismatched parents have been healthy and strong enough to sever their troubled relationship.

Two types of family environment are conducive to the development of psychiatric disorder in a child—whether his parents are divorced or not. The first is the presence of significant psychiatric disturbance in either or both of the parents. The second is parental misguidance. Of course, both may be present together and at times may not be readily distinguishable.

Whereas psychiatric disorder often requires specific treatment, the problems which arise from misguidance can often be alleviated and even avoided by appropriate instruction.

It is the aim of this book, through the guidance it offers the child, to relieve and avert some of the psychiatric difficulties that arise primarily from parental inexperience, naiveté, and misguidance. Although this book may also serve to mitigate and prevent some of the difficulties caused by parental psychiatric illness, the author is well aware that, at best, it can play only a limited role in this regard, for the disturbances which are so engendered usually **17** require more intensive approaches than just information and guidance.

Though written for the child and designed to be read by him, alone or along with a parent, some of the advice given here should be of value to parents as well in dealing with the problems discussed.

Above all, the book is based on the premise that some of the disturbances which children of divorced parents suffer result from the fact that their parents, often with the best intentions and even supported by professional authority, are not *appropriately* truthful about their divorce to their children. Note that I use the word *appropriately* because I do not believe that parents' lives should be an open book to their children. Parents have a tendency to hide from their children things which they have a right to know, things which, if disclosed, would be psychologically beneficial. Such information is usually withheld because the parents consider that its divulgence would be psychologically deleterious to their children.

Children are far less fragile in this regard than most parents realize, and they are much more capable of accepting painful realities than is generally appreciated. What is more difficult for them to handle (and this is true for adults as well) are the anxieties associated with ignorance and parental furtiveness, for then fantasy runs free and their worst anticipations can neither be confirmed nor refuted. Half-truths produce confusion and distrust, whereas truth, albeit painful, engenders trust and gives the child the security of knowing exactly where he stands. He is then in a better position to handle situations effectively.

The primary purpose of this book is to help children get along better with their divorced parents. Its main intent is not to counsel such parents on how to handle their children, although many things mentioned here may be helpful to them as well. In the many books and articles advising divorced parents how to handle their children two suggestions are frequently given to which I take exception. These recommendations have often served to aggravate rather than alleviate a child's difficulties.

The first is that parents should be extremely careful to impress continually upon the child that the absent parent (most often the father) still loves him despite the fact that he has left the household. The rationale for this is that it is important for the child to feel loved by the parent who is no longer in the home. It is certainly true that this is the case for the majority of absent parents, and in such situations this advice is appropriate and valid.

But what about the father who, living in the vicinity, hardly ever sees his child, or the father who abandons his family and is not heard from again for several years, if ever? What of the mother who runs off and forsakes her children? Do these parents love their children? I hardly think so. Should these children be told that their parents still love them? I say No. A child who is told that such a person still loves him cannot really believe it. The child senses the duplicity and loses trust in the parent who tells him what he knows is untrue. If a parent can allegedly love a child and yet never wish to see him again, the child then becomes confused about what love really is.

Such children are far better off when they are told that the absent parent has little, if any, love for them. This is *not* necessarily a reflection on the child. A parent's failure to love his child does not make the child unlovable, nor does it mean the child cannot be loved by someone else now or in the future. It does mean that the parent must have some serious defect in his personality (whatever his assets may be) which prevents him from loving **19** his own child. He is to be pitied if he is incapable of experiencing this great source of gratification. The child should be encouraged to seek love from those who will return it, for without reciprocity there can be no true love.

The second myth is that divorced parents should not criticize one another to the child. The rationale for this is that it is important to the child's healthy psychological development that he have respect and admiration for each of his parents. Only virtues are to be discussed.

Here, again, distrust and confusion are created. The child knows quite well that each of his parents believes the other to have serious personality flaws for why else would they be divorced? It's reasonable that a child whose parents speak only of the ex-partner's assets and merits should ask, "If he was so great, why did you divorce him?" Such a child already has enough trouble. He hardly needs the additional unnecessary problem of a distrustful attitude toward his parents. Moreover, his picture of the praised person will necessarily be grossly distorted, because he doesn't believe his primary source of information, and his fantasies can only be validated or refuted by his own, often primitive, observations.

The healthiest approach in such situations is to give the child an accurate picture of his parents as they really are: their assets and liabilities, their strengths and weaknesses. Like all humans, his parents are not perfect. He should respect each in those areas that warrant respect, and hold in low opinion those qualities which are not worthy of admiration. If a parent's defects far outweigh his strengths, so be it. This is not a reflection on the child. The child may suffer from having no admirable figure with whom to identify, but is this worse than emulating a contrived person whose assets exist only in words—words the child cannot fully believe?

ed by fiat or duplicity. The

him all the sordid details?"
best interests either. There
follow; but there are some
hip to the child must recog-
is behavior is judged by his
help his children perceive
nself and in his ex-spouse.
notorious lack of objectivity
cts, they should be cautious
wever, some situations are
it indicates a lack of inter-
en he exhibits genuine inter-
involvement, and it should
ther leaves her child under
ect, and it should be defined
of a new dress to buy her
concern, and her children

especially the "sordid" ones,
nce to the child. These are
the child should be told so.

The child also has a right to certain privacies of his own, and these should be respected by the parents. The details of a parent's behavior toward the child, no matter how contemptible, are *his business.* This must be faced by all concerned. These details should be discussed at a level comprehensible to the child and at a depth appropriate for his age. In such an atmosphere the child will know what to criticize and what to admire, what to love and what to dis-

21

like. He will then be far better prepared to handle those vicissitudes and paradoxes of life for which it is every parent's duty to prepare his child.

This book has been written to guide children in the handling of their divorced parents, not the reverse. There is, however, one recommendation I wish to present because it is so often omitted from the same manuals that provide the erroneous advice that has just been discussed. I single it out because it is probably not only the most simple and yet effective way of preventing pathological reactions in a child but also of alleviating them. I'm referring to the simple practice by parents of setting aside a few minutes each day to spend time alone with each of their children. This should be done at a time when the parent can direct his attention solely to the child and engage in meaningful conversations or mutually enjoyable experiences. The time need not be more than ten or fifteen minutes, but it should become a routine that takes high priority over other activities and obligations. Preferably, these periods should be at a time when both the parent and the child are least distracted by other concerns. Probably the most salutary thing that can happen during such time alone is that the two openly share deep thoughts and feelings of mutual concern. Such moments of rapport and empathic resonance provide the building blocks from which a healthy relationship is formed, and they are the most potent antidotes to those detriments in parent-child relationships which produce emotional disturbances.

In this book some of the common problems which confront children of divorced parents are presented to the child, along with suggestions of ways for him to solve, deal with, or adapt to his difficulties. My intent has been to discuss these questions as honestly as possible, at a depth comprehensible to, and at a reading level understandable to children from the middle grade school to the late junior high school periods. Adolescents will also find much here that will be of interest to them and will often read the book with enthusiasm, even though they may complain that it is too "childish" for them. The wise parent will recognize the teen-ager's fear of associating himself with anything smacking of child-hood but will not let such comments deter him from encouraging the adolescent to read it.

Some children may find portions of the material presented here anxiety-provoking, but, in my experience with children, this has not been the case. On the contrary, most of them have exhibited a deep and enthusiastic interest in this book. More often than not, the anxiety has been in the parents rather than in the child. The parent who decides beforehand that this book will be upsetting to his child may very well be depriving him of the opportunity to read what may be vitally helpful to him. Let your child be his own judge. Let his inner defenses be the final arbiters. The child who finds this material too painful will be a rare exception, but he will be able to protect himself by showing a lack of interest or by refusing to read the book. At worst, he will experience mild, transient anxiety, but he will not suffer any permanent psycholog-ical disability. Such disorders come about only through prolonged exposure to trauma and deleterious experiences. If your child seems hesitant, he should not be pressured. Instead, he should be told that he need not read the book if he does not wish to, and that it will be made available to him again should he change his mind.

Since the mother has custody of the children and the father visiting privileges in a great majority of divorces, this book is directed to the child in this category. However, those whose situation differs will also find much here that is applicable to them.

This book is not designed to be read in one sitting. Most children could not possibly absorb all of the information at once in a meaningful way. The Table of Contents is explicit enough for the child to select those topics which interest and concern him most. Little is lost if the book is not read in continuity. *It is hoped that the issues raised here will become points of departure for further discussions between parents and children.* Such conversations not only help resolve family problems, but also draw parents and children closer together, and such mutual inquiry and cooperative discussion help to reduce the parent-child schisms brought about by divorce.

INTRODUCTION FOR BOYS AND GIRLS

MY NAME IS Dr. Richard Gardner. I am a child psychiatrist. For those of you who don't know what that is, a child psychiatrist is a special kind of doctor who tries to help children who have troubles and worries.

Some of the children I see in my office have problems because their parents are divorced. These children often feel better about their worries after they learn from me some important things about their thoughts and feelings. I also talk with them about other things they can do to help themselves feel better.

In addition, these children have taught me many things about what they think and feel and what they can do to help themselves. I've written this book so that other children of divorced parents can be helped by the things these children and I have learned together.

I'd like to tell you a few things before we start talking about divorce. When something happens that's sad and painful, usually the best thing for you to do is to try to find out exactly what the trouble is. Then it is easier for you to decide what to do to help yourself feel better. Some children don't do this. Instead, they make believe that nothing's wrong, or they try to hide their sadness. When they do this, they are not trying to help themselves, and so their problems usually are not solved, and they may even

get worse. It's much better to know the truth about your problems than to hide from them, even though the truth can often be fright-

ening or painful. When you know the truth, you can often do something about your troubles. If you hide from the truth, you can do nothing about your problems, and so things usually get worse.

Some children do this with the problems they have about their parents' divorce. If such children were to stop hiding from their troubles and start trying to do something about them, they'd most often feel better about things. If you've been doing this, now's the time to stop!

In this book I give children advice about some of the things they can do. Many children whose parents are divorced are very unhappy, but they don't think that there's anything that they can do about their troubles. This is not so. In this book I'll tell you about some of the ways you can help yourself. I'll talk about many of the usual problems which the children of divorced parents have. Some will be like the ones you have, others will not. After each problem has been discussed, I tell you what things you can do to help yourself if you have that problem.

I'll talk about many problems. Don't try to read too much at once. If you like, look in the Table of Contents for the sections or chapters that interest you most, and read them first. Treat this book like an encyclopedia. You don't have to read the chapters in order. Read each part carefully and make sure you understand everything that's said. If you don't understand something, ask one of your parents to explain it to you. Don't be ashamed to ask the same question over and over again if you don't understand something. Most parents will be happy to explain things as many times as are needed to make them clear. Some children find it better to read this book along with a parent. In fact, I suggest that you discuss with your parents the things you read in this book as much as

possible.

If you read this book carefully, think about the things I have said, and try to do the things I have suggested, I think you'll feel better about your problems.

Bad horse or no horse at all?

1.

A FEW THINGS YOU SHOULD KNOW ABOUT DIVORCE

HOBSON'S CHOICE First I'd like to tell you about a man named Thomas Hobson. Thomas Hobson lived in England about four hundred years ago. At that time, there were no cars, so people rode around on horses. Mr. Hobson owned a large number of horses which he kept in a stable, and when people wanted horses, they'd rent them from him. Since people often spent a lot of time trying to decide which horse they wanted, Mr. Hobson made a new rule one day. This rule was that if you wanted a horse, you either had to take the one that was first in line or you got no horse at all. If you didn't like the horse that was first in line, your choice was between a horse you didn't like and no horse at all. This became known as "Hobson's choice." So today when someone has to choose between something he doesn't like and nothing at all, it's said that he has a Hobson's choice.

People who are unhappy about their marriage also have a Hobson's choice. They must choose between a bad marriage and no marriage at all. Some people stay in the unhappy marriage, and some decide to have no marriage at all. Those who stay in the bad **31** marriage often continue to fight and to be unhappy. Those who decide to get a divorce are usually sad and lonely at least for a time.

Most often parents are very sad about getting a divorce because they know how much it will hurt their children. But they are often in so much pain themselves, because of the terrible problems of the marriage, that they feel that they must get a divorce anyway. They do not wish to hurt their children, but they must think of their own feelings as well.

The child usually has no say in the matter. He must do what his parents decide. If a child were allowed to make the choice between an unhappy marriage with all its problems and a divorce with all its loneliness, most children would choose the unhappy marriage. This might not be the best choice. Often a child is better off when his parents get divorced than when they remain together and fight a lot.

What I have just said is very important. Psychiatrists have found that children who live in homes where the mother and father do not get along well get very upset and are likely to have many troubles and problems. Children whose parents get divorced often have fewer problems of this kind. Of course, it is best to live in a home where both parents are happy. But if this is not possible, you may be better off in a divorced home than in one where there is much fighting and unhappiness. Also when your parents are divorced, they can each try to find someone they can be happy with. Then you may have a happy home after all. Some parents are very unhappy in their marriage but don't get divorced because they think it would be worse for their children if they did so. This can be a mistake, for, as I have said, children are often better off when there's a divorce than when they have to live in an

32 unhappy home.

Bad marriage or no marriage at all?

FEELINGS CHILDREN HAVE AFTER THE DIVORCE Some children are surprised to find that after the divorce things are quiet in the house for the first time in their lives. It seems funny to say, but a child may have more time with his father after the divorce than he had when his father lived with him. Mothers and fathers often seem happier and are less fussy after a divorce.

There are some children, however, who are very, very sad right after the divorce. They may not wish to eat; they have trouble sleeping; they lose interest in playing and in their schoolwork, and they just mope around all the time. They may spend much of their time thinking of all the things they once did with their fathers.

They miss their fathers very much, and they keep wishing that their parents would get married again. They may cry a lot, and they may even feel ashamed because they cry. There is no reason to be ashamed about crying after your parents' divorce. Each time

The good old days with father.

you cry, you feel a little better about things. It's better to "get it off your chest," as the old saying goes. Most children who are unhappy this way gradually feel better as time goes on, and they get used to living without their fathers. That's a very important thing to remember: As time passes, the painful feelings about the divorce hurt less and less. It also makes a child feel better if he knows that his mother may someday marry again. If such a child makes friends with others, both of his own age and older, it can help make up for the loss of his father.

But some children spend most of their time hoping their parents will get back together even though their parents have told them many times that they won't marry again. As long as these children do this, they remain sad. When they finally stop hoping for something that cannot happen and start making up for the loss of their fathers by making friends with others, they begin to feel better.

2.

WHO'S TO BLAME?

THE WORDS "blame" and "fault" are often heard when there's a divorce in the family. Parents sometimes blame each other for the divorce, or they may blame the children, or sometimes each member of the family blames himself. In this chapter, I'm going to tell you about the different kinds of blame so that it will be clear to you when people really are at fault and when they are not.

YOUR PARENTS DID NOT GET DIVORCED BECAUSE YOU WERE BAD Sometimes a child thinks that his parents have gotten a divorce because he was bad. This is *not* the reason parents get divorced. They get divorced because they are unhappy with one another, and they no longer want to live together. It's *not* because their children have been bad.

Most often those who think that their parents got divorced because they were bad children are not even bad. Of course, like most children they do bad things once in a while. But they usually think their parents got divorced because they did certain things which were bad. This is not so. The divorce had nothing to do with the times that they were bad. These children sometimes think **37** that if they try very, very hard to be very, very good, their parents will marry again. I have never seen this happen. Since the divorce had nothing to do with the children's being bad, their being good cannot make their parents marry again.

If you're one of the children who think like this, ask your parents whether they got divorced because you were bad. I'm sure they'll tell you that badness had nothing to do with it. However, once in a while, a parent will tell a child that he did get divorced because the child was bad. If one of your parents says such a thing to you, do not believe it. If he says this, it usually means he has problems or troubles of his own that make it hard for him to see things the way they really are.

Children who think that their parents got divorced because they have been bad are often very sad about it. They may spend a lot of time thinking about how bad they were and trying to think of ways to be good so that their parents will marry again. Often these children do not spend much time with their friends and do not pay attention to their schoolwork.

Some children believe that the divorce was their fault because this makes them feel they can control the situation. Let me explain to you what I mean by this. As long as a child believes that he has caused his parents' divorce, it is easy for him to believe that he has the power to get his parents back together again. Believing it was his fault his parents got divorced gives the child a feeling of control over his parents' lives which he really doesn't have. By blaming himself for his parents' divorce in this way, he gives himself the hope that he will be able to get them to marry one another again.

It's best for children who think like this to stop trying to find ways to get their parents together again, to accept the fact that they will not get married again, and to realize that there's nothing they can do about it. It's something the children cannot control. There are many things in life which we cannot control, and a parent's divorce is one of them. Children must learn to accept this. Once they accept this fact, they must then try to make up for their loneliness by doing things with their friends, their classmates, and other people.

PARENTS' ACCIDENTS AND MISTAKES   Sometimes children think that the sadness and loneliness which resulted from their parents' divorce is the fault of one or both of their parents. In a way, it is the parents' fault, but most often they really do not wish to hurt their children, even though they have. I can make this clearer from the examples that follow.

This boy is working with his father in his father's tool shop. By accident, the father hits his son's finger with a hammer. The boy's finger hurts and feels sore. The father is very upset and says he is sorry, and the boy forgives him. Soon the boy's finger feels better, and they continue working.

Even though the boy's father hurt him by mistake, the father was to blame for the sore finger, and he felt very sad about having hurt his son.

This boy is also working with his father. His father gets angry at him and on purpose hits him on the finger with a hammer. This boy's finger also gets sore. The father does not say he is sorry. The boy does not forgive him. Instead, he stops working with his father in the shop for the rest of the day.

Now, both boys got sore fingers because their fathers hit them with a hammer. One boy's father hit him by accident and the other on purpose. In a way, both boys' sore fingers are their fathers' faults, but the father who did it by accident is far less to blame than the father who did it on purpose.

Because of their mistakes, divorced parents very often hurt their

children. Usually the parents think it was a mistake that they got married. They are sorry that their children have been hurt because of this mistake. This makes them very sad, but, like the man who accidentally hurt his son's finger, there is nothing they can do about it now.

THINGS PARENTS CANNOT CONTROL Sometimes a divorce is the result of things parents do which they cannot control.

This girl's father drank too much whiskey and beer. He got drunk often. Because of this he could not keep a job and take care of his family. Finally, his wife decided to get a divorce. He had tried very hard many times to stop drinking, but he just couldn't. It made him very sad to think that because he could not stop drinking his wife and children would be unhappy and lonely.

In a way, the divorce was the father's fault, but it was caused by something he was unable to stop. Many other problems that parents have which they cannot control also bring about divorce.

The parents who hurt children because they made the mistake of getting married and the parents who hurt children by problems and worries they cannot control are usually people who do not wish to harm their children. Although you may find yourself being angry at them, it's important to realize that you should also be sorry for them, because they too are very unhappy people. If you spend your time blaming them, you'll accomplish nothing.

THE PARENT WHO IS TO BLAME There are, however, a few parents who simply do not want to take care of their families, and so they just leave. I'm happy to say there are very few such parents. They didn't cause their children to be sad and lonely by mistake or because they couldn't help themselves. They are the kind of people who think of themselves and no one else. They are at fault. They leave on purpose, and it's hard to feel sorry for them when you're sad and lonely.

However, staying angry at such parents accomplishes nothing either. If you've tried to get such a parent to like you or to become interested in the family and it hasn't worked after a few tries, it's best just to forget about the whole thing as fast as you can and try to find others who do care. It's also important to remember that just because such a parent does not care for you does not mean no one ever will.

A FEW MORE THINGS ABOUT BLAME Often parents try to blame each other for the trouble in a marriage. Each one says it's *all, or mostly,* the other's fault. Each may say that the other did it on purpose, rather than by mistake or because he couldn't help it. Most often this is not true. Usually both have caused the trouble by mistakes or because of things they could not help. Often each parent has made mistakes, and each has problems and troubles which he cannot control very well. Parents, like many other people, feel better when they can blame others for the things they are ashamed of having done.

Sometimes a child thinks the divorce cannot be his parents' fault because he believes that they are perfect, and so he thinks it must be his fault. Such a child does not know the things I have just told you—how parents are not perfect, how they can make mistakes, and how they can do things which they do not like and yet cannot control. This does not mean that they are not any good at all, just that in certain things they do very poorly.

Blame is just a waste of time. It won't get your parents married again. Whether you blame yourself, your mother, or your father, nothing will change. The important thing is that you stop blaming people for things that happened in the past—things that cannot be changed—and start doing the things that will make the future happier.

Sometimes it's love.

Sometimes it's hate.

3.

THE LOVE OF A PARENT FOR A CHILD

"LOVE" IS A WORD that's used very often. It's a word that may be very confusing. One reason for this is that there are many different kinds of love. The kind of love I talk most about here is the love of a parent for a child. I do not talk about other kinds of love, such as the love between a mother and a father or the love of a child for a parent. "Love" can also be confusing because people often use this word when they mean something else. This is especially true of divorced parents. I'll say more about this later. In this chapter, I'll try to make things clear for you since many children of divorced parents are very, very confused about love.

MIXED FEELINGS An important thing to remember about love is that it doesn't stay the same all the time. No matter how much one person loves another, there are times when he has other feelings—feelings of dislike, anger, or even hate. Usually there's a mixture of feelings; sometimes it's love, sometimes hate, sometimes fear, sometimes loneliness, sometimes many other feelings **45**

Sometimes it's fear.

Sometimes it's loneliness.

46

as well. That's why I say that when one person loves another, he usually doesn't just have feelings of love, but a mixture of other feelings as well.

Some children think that it's wrong or bad to have mixed feelings toward their mother or father. They think that they should love their parents all the time. This is a wrong idea. If your mother does something which you don't like, you cannot *then* have a feeling of love. Usually at that time you'll have feelings of anger or even of hatred. This is normal, and it is how most children feel. When children are taught that it's very wrong to have angry or hateful feelings toward a parent, they often feel bad about themselves when they have such feelings. If such children knew what I'm telling you—that, at times, every child has feelings of hate and that it's normal to have such feelings mixed in with feelings of love—they would feel better about themselves.

In the same way, some children think parents shouldn't have mixed feelings. They think that a parent should only have feelings of love and nothing else. This cannot be. Even the most loving parents occasionally have feelings of hatred or anger toward their children. When a child does something that hurts a parent, it's normal for the parent to be angry at the child and for a short time not to feel love for him. Later, the parent will usually love the child again. When two people love, they love most of the time but usually not all of the time. Parents and children are no different in this way than are two friends. Sometimes they like being with one another, and sometimes they don't. Sometimes they love, and sometimes they do not. In a loving friendship there's much more of love than of other feelings.

Some people think that just because a person is a parent he loves his children all the time. This is not so. Although most parents **47** have mainly feelings of love, some parents have very few loving feelings toward their children, and a few have none at all. Fortunately, there are very few such parents.

HOW SOME PARENTS CONFUSE CHILDREN ABOUT LOVE It's very hard for a child to know whether his parents love him very much, very little, or not at all. Most parents love their children very much. Sometimes parents who love their children very little or not at all say that their love for them is very great. This can be very confusing. For this reason, what a person says is sometimes not a good way of learning whether he really loves you.

For a child whose parents are divorced, finding out how much a parent loves him is even more difficult. When a father leaves his family, his children often think that he left because he doesn't love them. Most often, this is not true. He left because he and their mother no longer wish to live together. The father usually loves his children very much, wishes he could live with them, and is very, very sorry to leave them. However, a few fathers who leave home really don't love their children, or they love them very little.

Sometimes a divorced father doesn't love his children, and yet the mother tells the children that he loves them even though she knows that he doesn't. She may have read that this is the best thing to say, and so she tells the children this because she thinks that it's better for them. She really thinks that she's doing the best thing for her children by telling them that their father loves them even though she knows that it isn't true. They would be better off if she told them the truth—whether it be that he loves them very little, that he does not love them at all, or that she does not know how much he loves them. Then they would trust their mother 48 more and be less confused about their father's love.

Some mothers never say bad things about the father because they think this will make the children keep on loving him even after the divorce. To do this, such mothers often have to tell their children things that they know are not true and hide from their children the things that are wrong with their father. If your mother does this, it's because she thinks that it's better for you not to know about your father's faults. She may even have read that she should never say bad things to you about your father, or she may think that you can only love a person who is perfect. But no one is really perfect, and when we love someone, it usually means that we love him even though some of the things he does and says are wrong or bad. Everybody has both good and bad parts. When we say we love someone, it means that there are more things we like about him than dislike.

If your mother does this, it would be better if she honestly told you some of the good things about your father along with some of the things that are wrong with him. Then you would know what to like and what not to like about him, what to love and what not to love, and when he is loving and when he is not. When a mother doesn't tell her children any of the bad things about their father, but speaks about him only as if he were perfect, her children may ask, "If he's such a great person, why did you divorce him?"

This does not mean she has to tell you all about your father's faults. Some things are personal. Just as you have some personal thoughts and feelings which your mother has no right to know about, she has a right to some of her own. These personal things usually are about the divorce. She may tell you about some of these things, but it is her right not to talk about others.

I have been discussing mainly a mother's hiding the father's faults from her children. Fathers may also act this way, and they may try to tell their children that the mother is perfect when they know she isn't. It's wrong for a father to do this for the same reasons that it's wrong for a mother to do this.

Some parents think that if they admit their own faults to their families, their children will either love them less or will not love them at all. Such mothers and fathers believe that their children will love them only if they are perfect. They will, therefore, try to hide their faults from their children. But no one is perfect. Such a parent doesn't realize that if a person has a *few* faults and he is willing to admit them, his children will have *more* love and respect for him, not less. We usually admire someone who is strong enough to admit his faults. It is only when a parent has very big faults that a child loses respect and love for him.

HOW TO FIND OUT IF SOMEONE LOVES YOU Suppose a parent leaves the home never to return again. Suppose he says that he loves you when he doesn't. Suppose divorced parents never, or hardly ever, say bad things about each other in front of their children. Then how can a child find out how much he is loved?

If this is your problem, one thing you can do is to tell your parents some of the things you've just read. Maybe they'll agree that they've been mistaken in hiding certain things from you and will then tell you things that can help you decide how much they love you. If they do tell you new things, it may take a long time—many weeks or even many months—before you can decide for yourself how your parents really feel about you, but you will start to find out whether they love you very much, very little, or not at all.

One way to tell how much a parent loves you is to find out how often he wants to be with you. This doesn't mean that a person loves you only if he wants to be with you all the time. It only means that the person *tries* to be with you as often as he can. A father usually has to work all day and a mother has to take care of the house, and they both have to do many other things too. But when these other things *always* seem to come first, when you *always* seem to come last, then it's possible that this parent hasn't much love for you. When a divorced father who lives close by hardly ever comes to visit, it may mean he doesn't love his child very much.

Another way to decide how much a parent loves you is to see how much he goes out of his way to help you when you're in trouble or how much concern and sympathy he shows when you're sick, hurt, or in trouble. The loving parent will make a great effort to help you when you need it, and he will be upset and sympathetic when you're having difficulty.

51

One more way to tell whether you're loved is to see how pleased your parents are with the things you learn to do. Do they smile with pleasure when you show them some new thing you've learned or done? If they look bored or answer most often with a grunt or mumble, then they may not love you very much.

Still another way is to see whether they're proud of you. Loving parents often want their friends to meet their children, and they are also proud to tell people about the good things their children have done. If they never, or hardly ever, do these things, it may be that they do not love you very much.

A further way to find out if they love you is to see if they enjoy doing things with you. It doesn't matter *what* so much—it's just doing things together that are enjoyable. There's not much love if a parent has little desire to do things with you.

If a parent gets angry or fussy with you even a few times a day, this doesn't mean that he does not love you. A few times a day is normal. We all get angry at one another once in a while no matter how much we love. When a parent is angry with you *most* of the time, every day, then most likely that parent has little, if any, love for you.

Another way to tell is to see how much your parent likes to hold you or touch you. Of course, as you get older, there's less and less of this. But loving parents like to touch their children often, even if only for a second or two.

Love is a very complicated thing, and there are still other parts of it I haven't talked about. It's often a very hard thing for a child to understand. It's best to discuss all the things I have just told you carefully with an adult to be sure that you haven't made any mistakes, for there are some children who, after reading what I've

just said, may decide that a parent doesn't love them when he really does. These children just haven't understood clearly what I've said.

THINGS YOU CAN DO WHEN A PARENT DOES NOT LOVE YOU Suppose that after reading these things and discussing them with an adult, you find out that one or even both of your parents doesn't love you very much. What does that mean, and what can be done about it?

First of all—and this is very important—it does not mean that you are no good or that *no one* can ever love you. If a parent doesn't love you, that is sad for him because he loses out on the fun of loving, and loving someone is fun. If he doesn't love you, his very *own* child, there's something very wrong with him. It does not necessarily mean there is something wrong with you. I repeat, if a parent doesn't love you, it does not mean that you are not good enough to be loved or that you are very bad or that no one will ever be able to love you. It just means that there is something wrong with your parent that makes him unable to love his own child.

It's also very sad for a child to find out that he isn't loved by a parent. He feels cheated, and he wishes he were like kids who are lucky enough to have two loving parents. But to mope around and be unhappy accomplishes nothing. It just makes the sadness stay. Only by doing something can you help the unhappiness go away.

Now what can be done?

First, to get a parent to love you when he does not is very hard. Sometimes a child does certain things which make his parent love him less. Often, discussions with the parents will help the child learn what these things are, and if he can stop doing these things, the parent may love him more.

If this doesn't work, the best thing to do is to stop trying to get the parent's love. Some children try for years to get love from a parent who just cannot or will not give it. This just makes these children sadder and angrier. It is, in such cases, best to accept the fact that you cannot get their love and to start trying to get love and friendship from other people. Sometimes there are relatives or friends, old and young, who will love you. Two things are important to remember here. 1) If a parent doesn't love you, this does not mean that you are no good or that no one else can love you, and 2) if a parent doesn't love you, you shouldn't waste too much time trying to change him. Look for love somewhere else.

There's an old saying, "Don't try to squeeze water out of a stone." For those of you who have never heard this saying or do not understand it, it means that if somebody cannot or will not give you something, then you should forget about it. Don't keep trying to get it because to do so would be like "trying to squeeze water out of a stone." If you are looking for water, go where the water is and don't go to stones. If you're looking for love, go to the person who'll give it to you, not to the person who won't.

Go where the water is.

Don't go to stones.

4.

ANGER AND ITS USES

THE USE OF ANGER People have many different kinds of feelings, and each one comes out in its own special way.

Happiness is the feeling that comes out when things go well for us.

Sadness is what we feel when things go bad.

We feel *fear* when something scares us.

Anger is the feeling that comes out when we want something that we cannot have or which we think we cannot have.

This boy is angry because he wants ice cream and his mother says that he may not have it because it's almost time for supper.

Anger has a use. It helps you try to get what you want but think you cannot have. Sometimes it works, and you do get what you want. Sometimes it doesn't help, and then you still don't get the thing you want.

This boy's friend took his toy boat, and it made him angry. While he was still mad, he grabbed the boat back and told the other boy he had better not do that again.

This worked, and the other boy let him alone. The anger helped the boy get back his toy, and then he was no longer angry.

This girl was playing with a boy who was bigger than she. He took her ball, and while she was mad she tried to grab it back. But because the boy was bigger and stronger, she could not get it away from him, so the anger did not help, and she continued to feel sad and angry because she no longer had her ball.

As you can see, anger sometimes helps you get what you think you cannot have, but it doesn't always work. Sometimes it does, and sometimes it doesn't. One thing is sure. If you don't use your anger to help you, there's less chance you will get what you thought you could not have.

This girl was playing with a friend who took one of her dolls. Although she was angry, she did not show it. She didn't try to get her toy back, so the friend kept the doll, and the girl was very sad. If she had shown that she was angry, she might have gotten it back.

Anger comes when you cannot have something that you want. You can use it to help you get that thing. Sometimes it helps, and

sometimes it doesn't. When it does work, you are no longer angry. That is the best way to get rid of anger. When it doesn't work, then you are still angry for a while at least. It's better to let it out and use it to help you because then you have a better chance of getting what you thought you could not have.

Now what can you do if you've let out your anger, have tried to use it to help you get something, and you still cannot get the thing?

SUBSTITUTES FOR THE THING YOU WANT   One thing to do is to stop trying to get that thing and try to get something else in its place, something which may be just as good or almost as good. This new thing is called a *substitute*.

This boy wants some cake. His mother says there is none in the house. He's very angry because he cannot have the cake he wants,

and he'll continue to be angry as long as he keeps trying to get cake when there is none. Then he decides that candy will do just as well or is almost as good. When he gets the candy, which is the substitute, he's no longer angry.

Most children of divorced parents are angry because they want their parents to get married again, and they won't. The parents say that they were divorced because they no longer loved each other and were unhappy together, and therefore they will not marry again. Such children will be angry as long as they keep trying to get their parents together again. They'll be angry as long as they keep hoping that their parents will change their minds. They don't stop hoping and trying, and as long as they do this, they'll be angry.

This girl kept having temper tantrums because her father hardly ever visited her. When she finally realized that the temper tantrums were not getting him to visit her more often, she stopped having them. She then started to play with other children more, and this helped her miss her father less. The other children were a substitute for her father.

She felt better then and was less angry.

65

CHANGING YOUR MIND ABOUT THE THING YOU WANT Sometimes when a child is angry because he wants something he cannot have, he talks to his parents about it and learns that it's not proper, right, or fair for him to have the thing. If he stops wanting it, he will then no longer be angry. So if you change your mind about wanting something, you will no longer be angry. It's very important, therefore, to talk to your parents about your anger and to see whether or not you're *right* in wanting the thing.

This girl was angry because her mother had a date one or two nights a week. After they talked about it, the girl gradually realized that her mother had the right to have fun too. She was then less angry.

She was angry . . .

. . . until she understood.

CHANGING YOUR MIND ABOUT THE PERSON YOU'RE ANGRY AT Sometimes a divorced mother will keep telling her child that his father hates him and that she is the only one who loves him, the only one he can trust. She may make the child think that his father is secretly his enemy and that he will be very cruel to him if he has a chance. Then when the child is alone with his father, and the father does something the child doesn't like, the child thinks this is proof that his father really hates him and that his mother is right. Because he is alone with his father, he becomes frightened, and he may get very, very angry because he is afraid that his father will do horrible things to him.

Sometimes a divorced father will tell his child that his mother really hates him; so each time the child's mother does something he doesn't like he thinks this is proof that his father is right.

It's important for such children to remember that divorced parents often say terrible things about one another which may not be true. Each one tends to see the other as being hateful to both themselves and the children. If a mother tells a child that his father hates him or if a father tells a child that his mother hates him, the child should usually not believe this because most often it's not true. It's very, very rare that a parent truly hates his own child. Of course, a good parent, at times, punishes his child or is strict with him. This just means that the parent is interested and loving. It doesn't mean that he hates the child.

Therefore, if a child is angry at a parent because he thinks that the parent hates him, he will be much less angry when he comes to realize that this is hardly ever true.

YOU'RE NOT BAD IF YOU GET ANGRY Some parents think that it's a terrible thing for a child to have angry feelings. Even if the parents are divorced, they don't think it's right for their child to be angry at them. This is wrong. But parents are not perfect, and they sometimes have foolish ideas. They may say things such as "What a terrible child you are to say such angry things to your mother. You shouldn't even *think* such things." Or the parents may not know what I've told you about mixed feelings, and they may tell the child that he's very bad if he doesn't love his parents *all* the time. In this way, the child is made to feel very bad about himself when he gets angry at them, even if it is only once in a while. He may not know that all children get angry at their parents at times, especially when there has been a divorce.

Some children feel so bad about getting angry that they are afraid to talk about it even though it happens only once in a while. Others are so scared of their anger they won't even let themselves think about it! They've come to think that only the worst, most terrible children ever think angry thoughts about their parents. They don't know that most children get angry at their parents a lot and that the only ones who don't are those who have been taught that it's a terrible thing, which it isn't.

Because these children don't let out their anger, they do not get many of the things they might get if they did let it out.

This girl has never told her father how angry she gets when he's late for his Sunday visits. She thinks it's horrible to be angry

at your father. So he keeps coming late, and she keeps getting more and more angry. Not only does she feel terrible about herself when she's angry, but because she also doesn't speak up, her father keeps coming late, and she has less time with him.

This girl told her father how angry it made her when he came late. He said children should never get angry at their parents. She answered, "That's wrong; as long as you keep coming late, I'll be angry." Her father thought about what she had said, agreed that

Now he comes on time. She's not angry anymore.

she was right, and started to come on time. Now she's no longer angry.

This girl told her father how angry she was about his coming late. She told him that she would continue being angry as long as he continued to be late. He answered that she was wrong to be angry at him no matter what he did because a child should never be angry at her parent. He still kept coming late. She slowly learned that although her father had many right ideas, he also had

71

She has fun instead of waiting.

some wrong ideas about anger, so she stopped trying to change his mind because it was no use. She also came to understand that he didn't love her enough to want to spend much of his time with her. Now she does other things instead of waiting. She does not count on him as much as before, and so she's less angry.

ANGRY THOUGHTS CANNOT HARM ANYONE All children, when they are very young, think that anything they wish can come true and that anything they think can come true. As they get older they learn this is not so, that thinking alone does not make something happen and wishing doesn't always make it so. But there are some children who have grown older and have not learned this. They still believe that just *thinking* something will happen can *make* it come true. Some of these children believe that if they think an angry thought about someone, what they think will actually happen.

This girl was so angry at her father for getting a divorce that she kept having thoughts that he would get sick or have an accident. She became very frightened about these thoughts because she was afraid they would come true. She not only became scared of saying angry things but even thinking them. She doesn't know that thinking something, no matter how hard you think it, cannot make the thing come true.

Once in a while a child is very angry at a parent and wishes he were sick or dead. Then something really does happen to him. This does not mean that her thoughts made the person become sick or die. The person died from sickness or an accident, not from the child's wish or thought. The person would have gotten sick or would have died anyway, and it had nothing to do with the child's thoughts. In fact, no matter how much a person may wish someone **72** sick or dead, the wishing cannot make it happen.

For this reason some children are afraid to say or even think angry thoughts. When they learn that thoughts alone cannot make a thing happen, they are sometimes able to let their anger out and use it to help them get some of the things they want.

ANGRY THOUGHTS AND ANGRY FEELINGS Anger has two parts: angry *thoughts* and angry *feelings*. It's important for you to understand the difference between them.

When you're angry at someone, you may have thoughts about the person being hurt or even killed, or bad words may come into your mind. Angry feelings are the feelings that go along with these thoughts. Usually it's best to let the angry feelings out but **73** *not* to *say* your every exact angry thought, for this may hurt people's feelings and get you in trouble. It's often best to do this by using words which are more polite than those which first came to your mind. The important thing is to let the anger help you get what you want.

This girl was very angry because her father was late for his Sunday visits so often. Sometimes she'd get so angry at him that she'd wish he'd get hit by a car. Many bad words came into her mind too. All these thoughts were there, along with her angry feelings.

One day she told her father that it made her very angry when he was late. She felt angry as she said this. She was letting out her angry feelings. She did not tell her father that she wished he would get hit by a car, nor did she tell him of the bad language that had come into her mind. She knew it would hurt him if she were to say these things, and besides her father had told her that it was often all right to use such words to one's friends but not to one's parents or teachers. Her father then made sure that he was on time, and the girl no longer had these angry thoughts and feelings.

IMPORTANT THINGS TO REMEMBER ABOUT ANGER   Before I finish this chapter, I would like to repeat a few of the things I have said to be sure they are clear in your mind.

1. Anger is the feeling people have when they want something they think they cannot have. For this reason children whose parents are divorced get angry, for they usually want their parents to be together, and they cannot have this.

2. Anger can help you get certain things that at first you thought you couldn't have. The anger goes away when you get what you want.

3. If it's not possible to get the thing you want, then the anger may still go away if you get something else instead. This other thing is called a *substitute*.

4. Every person gets angry at times, and you are not terrible for having angry thoughts and feelings even toward your parents.

5. Having angry thoughts toward someone will not cause that person harm.

6. Anger has two parts: angry thoughts and angry feelings. Most often it's useful to let out the angry feelings. Often it's better not to say exactly what one's angry thoughts are, but to say more polite things instead, which will help you get what you want.

5.

THE FEAR OF BEING LEFT ALONE

THE ONE-EYED MAN Most people who have two eyes do not go around being scared that something will happen to their sight. If a man with two eyes does have an accident or a sickness that destroys one of his eyes, he still has the other eye, and so he can still do most things.

However, when a man has only one eye, he usually worries about it, takes care of it quite well, and is careful that nothing happens

to it. Because if something were to happen to the one eye that he has left, he would be completely blind.

Children with only one parent are often like a one-eyed man. When they had two parents, they did not worry about having only one. But when they're left with only one parent, they're very frightened. They worry that if something happens to that one parent, they'll be all alone, and they fear that terrible things will happen to them.

They may be afraid that they'll have no place to live, that they'll be without food or clothing, or that they'll have no one to take care of them. They may even be afraid that they will die.

There is no good reason for a child whose parents are divorced to have such worries, for there are many things that can be done to solve their problems.

YOU STILL HAVE TWO PARENTS   First of all, children whose parents are divorced still have two parents. Although the parents are living apart, they usually are both still alive, and they are usually still able to take care of their children. If something should happen to one parent, a child could still live with the other one.

This girl's parents were divorced, and she lived with her mother. She was very sad when her mother died. She now lives with her father. Because her father has to work to provide the things she needs, she is cared for by a nice lady who lives in her father's house. The woman keeps house for them, and she is called a house-

keeper. Naturally, the girl would like it better if her mother were alive, but she is not as unhappy as she had thought she would be at first.

However, it sometimes happens that a child cannot live with either of his parents. This doesn't happen very often, but when it does, a number of other things are possible.

LIVING WITH RELATIVES AND FRIENDS   Most children have relatives with whom they can live. Usually an aunt, uncle, cousin,

grandparents, or even a good friend of their parents will take care of them. This may not be as good as living with one's own parents, but it's one of the ways that a child can be taken care of. If you have many relatives or if your parents have many good friends, its likely that if something happens to your parents, you'll be able to live with one of these people.

Some children are worried about where they would go if something happened to both their parents, but they feel better after talking to their parents and finding out what plans have been made for them. It's a good idea to ask your parents what they've planned for you in case something should ever happen to both of them. If they have not thought about these things, it would be a good idea for you to ask them to do so. It's important for you to know whom you would live with if something happened to one or both of your parents.

What happens if a child cannot live with his parents or with their friends or his relatives? There are other places he can go to live where he will be cared for.

BOARDING SCHOOLS One such place is a boarding school. Boarding schools are places where children live and attend school. They have school buildings there in addition to the houses where the children live and eat. There are also places for sports and games. These are all together in one place, which is usually in the country. A few, however, are in the city. There are grown-ups there who like children. Often there are married people too, who enjoy taking care of the children at the boarding school as if they were their own. Everything is all together, so a child gets to know his teachers much better. Frequently, the teachers also live on the school grounds. Some children who did not get along well with **81**

their parents become very friendly with the teachers and the other people at the boarding school. They may become so fond of some of them that they even grow to love them. When this happens, children are quite happy in the boarding school.

There are many boys and girls at boarding schools all the time, and so a child never has to be alone if he doesn't wish to be. Many children of divorced parents live in places where there are few, if any, children with the same problems that they have, but at a boarding school they can usually find many other children of divorced parents. This helps them feel less different from others and less sad about their parents' divorce.

Boarding schools have visiting days on which a child can be visited by his parents, other relatives, or friends. Also there are times when the child can leave the school to visit people. But as pleasant as such a school can be, it is still not as good as living at home with two happy, loving parents. Still, if your parents are divorced, this may be the best choice you have.

Most children are sad when they first go to boarding school. They think they are being sent there because they've been bad or because their parents don't love them. Usually this isn't so. Most children are sent because it's the best thing their parents can do for them. If they lived at home, they might not get all the attention and care they deserve and need.

It's sad to say, but some parents send their children to boarding schools because they do not love them very much and they just want to get rid of them. Fortunately, there are very few such parents. Such children, of course, are very unhappy. They may even think this means they are no good at all and that no one will ever love them. Many of these children can find friends at the boarding school, and this often helps them feel better about themselves. It's very important for these children to remember that just because their parents don't love them very much, this doesn't mean that they're no good or that no one else will ever love them.

Many children are frightened when they first go to boarding school, but new things are always scary, even for grown-ups. However, these children usually get to know the place, and they like it after a while. Then they are no longer frightened.

FOSTER HOMES   Next, I would like to tell you about foster homes. When a child cannot live with one or both of his parents, he sometimes goes to live in a foster home where he can be cared for while he is growing up. In such homes there is usually a mother and   **83**

father who might have children of their own. They may even have one or more children of other people living with them as well. The children of other people in these homes are called foster children. Usually the parents in these homes have great love for children, and their foster children are very happy with them. Some children of divorced parents are happier in foster homes than they would be if they lived with either of their own parents.

Sometimes, however, foster homes are not very pleasant. The foster mother may love her own children more than she loves her

foster children. She may be taking care of the foster children just for the money she is paid. When this happens, the foster child can often get moved to another foster home by telling the people who sent him there how unhappy he is. If this does not work, then the child has little choice but to stay until he is older.

Again, it's important to remember that there are always things such a child can do to help himself feel better. He can become friends with children and adults outside the foster home. He can look forward to the day when he will be older, when he will be bigger and stronger. Then he'll be able to do many of the things he now wants to do but cannot, and he'll be able to find many friends who'll like and love him, and whom he can like and love in return. If, however, he spends his time thinking that the world will never be a good place for him no matter what he does, he may not try to find the good things in life that are to be had by almost everyone who'll work for them.

And so you can see, no child is left alone without food, clothing, a house to live in, or people to take care of him. Everybody is taken care of in some way. Such care may not be as good as that which a parent would give him, but it's usually not as bad as children sometimes fear it will be.

6.

HOW TO GET ALONG BETTER WITH YOUR DIVORCED MOTHER

CHILDREN WHO LIVE with their divorced mothers, and whose fathers live elsewhere, have special problems that other children do not have. In this chapter, I tell you about some of these difficulties and some of the things you can do about them.

WISHING YOUR MOTHER WOULD GET MARRIED AGAIN Many children of divorced parents wish their mothers would marry again. Most of them wish it would be to their father, and if not to him, then to another man. These children keep asking their mothers over and over when they're going to get married again. This usually upsets the mother and makes her feel bad about the divorce. It would be a great mistake if such a mother were to marry a man she did not love just because she thought this would make her child happier. If she does marry for this reason, the child is usually not happier, but sadder, because the mother isn't happy. She gets angry easily, is fussy, and there's much fighting in the house because she's married to a man she doesn't love. Remember, it's more often better to live with no father than to live with one whom your mother doesn't love. **87**

ACTING TOO GROWN-UP WITH YOUR MOTHER All children of divorced parents have to do certain grown-up things that other children don't have to do. It's often necessary for them to help their mothers more than other children do with shopping, baby-sitting, cleaning, and other jobs around the house. This is fine and healthy because it's good for a child to do a certain amount of adult work. However, some mothers, because they are very lonely, try to make their sons take the place of their husbands or their daughters take the place of their adult women friends.

Such a mother may want her son to go with her when she visits friends and relatives and to act more like a husband than a son. She may ask his advice about things she would have usually asked her husband's advice on, and she may tell him personal things that mothers usually don't tell their sons. She may want him to act like a grown-up, going with her to the movies and to other places. Such a mother may hold hands with her son and kiss him a lot. She may even want him to sleep in the same bed she does.

It's natural and normal for young children to spend a little time in bed with their mothers, especially right before they go to sleep. Many small children enjoy climbing into their mother's bed early in the morning to be cuddled. However, some mothers want their children to spend hours doing this, and they may even want their son to sleep with them all night. When such things happen, the boys often have trouble when they grow up and meet girls whom they might date and marry. It's a very bad idea for a boy to do all these things with his mother. He should try not to do them even if she asks. He should talk to her about how bad these things could be for him and tell her that she should find a grown-up man instead.

88   There are also boys who try to act like their divorced fathers.

They want to do with their mothers many of the grown-up things I have just talked about. To do adult things once in a while is good for all children, but doing them too often may cause the child trouble. He may have difficulty with his friends, who will not like him because he acts like a grown-up so often. And when he gets older, he may still have trouble with boys and girls his age.

89

Some mothers, because they are lonely, try to turn their daughters into grown-up friends. They ask them for advice and try to get them to visit with older friends and relatives, just as they would if the child were an adult. Such a mother may ask a daughter to call her by her first name. Or she may ask her daughter to take most of the care of the younger children in the family. When this happens, it's not a good idea for the daughter to do all these things. She should suggest that her mother find friends her own age.

ACTING LIKE A BABY WITH YOUR MOTHER Some mothers try to keep their children babies instead of helping them act bigger and more grown-up as they get older. They always worry whether their children are dressed warmly enough or whether they have eaten well, and they hardly ever let their children do the jobs around the house that other children their age have to do. They may keep their children at home while others are outside playing. This is bad, and these children should try to do everything they can to stop their mothers from babying them.

Some children, saddened by the divorce, try to get extra attention and care by acting younger than they really are. Some mothers go along with this and baby the child. A good mother will not baby her child no matter how much he wants her to, for she knows the best thing she can do for her child is to help him grow up. She knows other children will not want to play with him if he is babyish, and that later on in life he may become sad and lonely and have other troubles as well.

Remember, the best thing you can do for yourself is to *act your age*. Don't go back to being a baby, no matter how good it may feel at times, and don't try to be too grown-up.

THE "GOOD-GUY" FATHER AND THE "MEAN OLD" MOTHER

When a father lives at home, both he and the mother join the children in doing fun things like going on picnics, or going to the beach, the circus, or the movies. They also do things together which may not be so much fun, such as making you dress, pick up your clothes, or come in from play. Both also punish you when you do the wrong things and praise you when you do the right things.

When parents get divorced, it may seem that during the week the mother has to do all the things that aren't fun, and that on weekends the father gets to do most of the fun things. Because your father does not see you so often, he tries to do the nicest things. Your mother, however, must make sure you do *everything* correctly, such as eating on time, going to school, and sleeping

enough. Because of this, a child may look upon his father as the "good guy" and his mother as a "mean old lady."

Such a child does not see things the way they really are. He sees his mother as being worse than she really is. If she were with him only on weekends, she too would try to do the fun things. Such a child also sees his father as being better than he really is. If he *were* really a good father, he would also do the things that are not fun with his child. In the next chapter, I discuss these things and point out that some fathers, by spending most of their time on amusements and presents, cause their children to miss out on many other wonderful things.

WHEN YOUR MOTHER TALKS ABOUT YOUR FATHER Some mothers seem to be perfectly all right except when they talk about their divorced husbands. Then they get angry and upset, and the things they say may not all be correct. If your mother does this, she may say bad things about your father which are not true, or she may say that he hates you when he really doesn't. At these times, it's better not to take what she says too seriously. You have to ask yourself at such times if your father really is the way she says he is. Have you seen him do the bad things she says he does? Have you heard him say the bad things she says he says? You also have to use your own opinions to help you decide whether she is right or wrong. When she's less upset, she'll say things you can trust. Even parents who are not divorced have times like these, and it's best for a child to know when his parent is in this kind of mood.

IF YOUR MOTHER WORKS Sometimes a mother has to work so that her children can have good food, clothing, and a nice place to live. If a mother who works is also divorced, her children are even

more unhappy and lonely because they do not see much of their father and they see little of their mother as well. If your mother works for these reasons, it doesn't help things if you're always telling her not to work. She probably would prefer not to work, but she has to do so if she is to buy you the things you need.

Some children think that if their mothers loved them, they would not work. This usually isn't so. They work because they need the money for you, and they work because they do love you. If they didn't love you, they wouldn't work to be able to buy you the things you need.

Some mothers have enough money to buy the things they need for themselves and their children, but they work anyway because they enjoy their work or find it very interesting. It makes them happier, at least part of the time, if they work. If they were not to work, they might be very unhappy. But their children sometimes think their mothers do not love them very much. This is usually not so. Just because a mother wants to spend some of her time doing what she enjoys, it does not mean that she doesn't love her children. Children have the right to their fun and interests, and mothers have the right to theirs. In fact, since working makes such mothers happier, they are often more loving toward their children.

Children whose mothers work often find that if they join school clubs or play with other children after school, they are not as sad and lonely about their mothers' working.

YOUR MOTHER'S DATING Now I'll talk about your mother's dating. For those of you who don't know what "dating" means, your mother's going out with a man is what's called dating. The man is called your mother's "date." People do many things on dates. Sometimes they eat dinner in a restaurant or see a movie or a show, or they may go dancing or meet with friends.

Most of the time children do not go along on dates although they often would like to. Your mother's dates are private. You don't have the right to know everything about her dates—whom she goes out with, where she goes, or what she does. Just as you have thoughts and feelings and things that you do which are private, so has your mother the right to her own privacy. It's normal for a child to be curious about and interested in these things, but it's also normal for her not to tell you everything about them.

Mothers have dates for a number of reasons. Since your mother has been divorced, she's probably been sad and lonely. By dating,

she can become less lonely, and she can have good times which will help her feel less sad. Also, just as you have time for your fun, your mother's dates are her fun times. Just as you like to do things without your mother even though you may love her very much, she too likes to do things without you at times. This does not mean that she doesn't love you. She often hopes that, by dating, she'll be able to meet someone whom she can love and marry. She hopes also that the man she finds will love her children too.

Many children think that a man and a woman decide to get married very soon after they've met each other. Some children believe that people decide this in a few minutes, but this is not true. People usually take many months and sometimes even a few years before they decide whether or not they're going to get married. Since this is such an important decision, they want to be sure they know each other quite well and that they love each other enough to want to live together for the rest of their lives. This is especially true of people who've been divorced. They have been hurt and disappointed because of a bad marriage, one in which love didn't last, so they try to be extra careful about marrying again and to be sure that the new marriage will be better.

Children, however, may not want them to wait so long. A child may keep asking his mother when she's going to get married, and he may try to get her to marry before she's sure that she loves the man she's going with. This is a very bad idea, for if a mother marries a man she doesn't love because she thinks this will help her children, things usually get worse because she then becomes unhappy and fussy.

Some children will ask each of their mother's dates if he's going to be their new father. This question usually makes both your mother and her date feel uncomfortable, and it doesn't help your

mother get married any sooner. In fact, it may make it take longer, for a man doesn't like to be pushed into marriage. If someone tries to force him—whether it's you or your mother—he may go away.

Because many children want a father very much, they hope each new date will become their new father. They are then very disappointed if their mother doesn't see the man again. It's important to remember that most mothers see many, many men before they meet the one whom they marry. And when they finally do meet him, they usually take a long time before they decide to marry him. If you keep hoping that each man will be your new father, you'll have many disappointments.

Often your mother can help solve this problem by not having

you meet each date but only those whom she likes a lot and sees often. If your mother does have you meet each date, you might ask her to help you by not doing this, and only introduce those she will be seeing often. In this way, you'll have fewer men to be disappointed about. However, you must remember that even then there will be disappointments. Also, if you try to get more fun out of your life as it is, you'll have less need to depend on a new father.

Remember, all the men your mother dates will be gone in time —except the one your mother marries. And some mothers never marry again. If you think that your life is being wasted without a father, you'll go around feeling sad and disappointed. However, if you try to do the best you can without one, to have the fun of friendships and the fun of learning and doing things, your life can still be happy.

Some children are just the opposite. They do not want their mothers to get married again. They're frightened of each new date, and they try to keep their mothers from going out. When they meet a new man, they are often nasty and mean to him. They fear

that if their mother got married, she would pay less attention to them and would love them less.

These children have the wrong idea about love. They think that their mother has only a certain amount of love. They think love's like a piece of pie, and that if she gives half to someone, then there's only half left. It's not that way at all. A person can love a number of people at the same time. In fact, love works just the opposite way: The more love you give, the more you're able to give. When a mother finds a nice man to love, she is better and more loving to her children. Many children do not realize that the happier their mother is, the happier they will be with her.

If such children are nasty and mean to each new man, they can scare him away. This may make it harder for their mother to marry again. If these children knew what I have just said—how they would probably be happier, not sadder, if their mothers married again—then they might not try to get rid of each new man.

Some children are jealous of the dates their mothers have. Their mother and her date go out alone together for an evening or a day, sometimes even for a few days. They may hug and kiss each other at times. These children should remind themselves that someday, when they grow older, they too will be able to meet someone who is nice, whom they can have all to themselves, and with whom they can do all the things that their mother is doing now.

TIME ALONE WITH YOUR MOTHER No matter how busy your mother may be, taking care of you or working or dating, there is one very important thing that she should take time out to do with you. Every day there should be time alone together, when your mother puts aside whatever she's doing and spends at least a few minutes alone with each of her children. This is best done at a time when she doesn't have too many things on her mind. During these times, you and your mother can talk about personal things, your problems, hopes, disappointments, and experiences, both happy and sad. Or you may play or read together, or discuss what you have done in school, or anything else of interest to you both.

If your mother is not doing this, see if you can get her to, because it's during these times alone together that you can really get close to your mother, and you can often avoid or solve many of your problems.

If you try to do the things I have told you in this chapter, I'm sure there'll be fewer problems between you and your divorced mother.

7.

HOW TO GET ALONG BETTER
WITH YOUR DIVORCED FATHER

MOST CHILDREN whose parents are divorced live with their mothers and visit their fathers at special times, such as weekends and holidays. A few children never, or hardly ever, see their fathers.

First, I'll talk about fathers who visit, and then about those who don't.

FATHERS WHO SPOIL THEIR CHILDREN Most fathers feel very bad about their divorce and are very sorry they are not living with their children. Because of this, they often try to make up for their absence by giving their children practically anything they want and spoiling them in many other ways. They may always be giving them presents, they may not punish or control their children when they need it, and they may try to spend all their time with them in doing one fun thing after another.

Although children most often think that this is a great way to spend a weekend, they don't realize that they're not getting certain things from their fathers which are even more important. Next I'll tell you about some of these things. **101**

FATHERS WHO DO NOT PUNISH OR DISCIPLINE   When children are not punished or disciplined the way they should be, they do not learn correct behavior. They then have trouble with other people they meet who will not let them get away with what their fathers allow.

When these brothers visited with their father on weekends, they never had to go to sleep on time, put away their toys, clean up after playing, wash their hands and face, comb their hair, or pick up their soiled clothing. When they broke things in his house, he never scolded or punished them. When they returned home after each visit, they had trouble getting along with their mother, who insisted on correct behavior. Also, their teachers wouldn't put up

with their horseplay and lack of discipline. They were so busy getting into trouble they didn't learn very much in school.

FATHERS WHO DO NOT MAKE CHILDREN DO THINGS ON THEIR OWN   Children whose fathers give them most of the things they ask for miss out on the fun of working to get these things themselves.

This boy's father bought him most of the toys he wanted. He got tired of each toy soon after he got it. He did not enjoy things very much and did not feel good about himself.

This boy's father bought him presents mainly for special occasions like birthdays and holidays. Otherwise, he had to buy things himself, by saving his allowance or from money he earned doing jobs like cutting grass. Instead of bringing him expensive toy boats and planes, his father bought him less-expensive toys or models which he could work on himself, sometimes with his father's help. This boy felt very good about the toys he got, enjoyed them a long time, and was proud of the things he made himself or bought with his own earnings. As a result, he felt very good about himself.

It is more fun doing something yourself than getting something after all the work has been done by someone else.

TOO MANY FUN THINGS, TOO FEW PERSONAL THINGS   A certain amount of time spent at places like a circus, zoo, amusement park, or movie is fun, normal, and healthy. However, some fathers spend most of their visiting time with their children at such places. Some of these children miss doing many of the little everyday things which are just as much fun, and are more important to a child if he is to grow up happily. These are things such as eating meals with him, taking walks with him, helping him clean and fix his car, and sharing with him the hundreds of other little things which happen all the time.

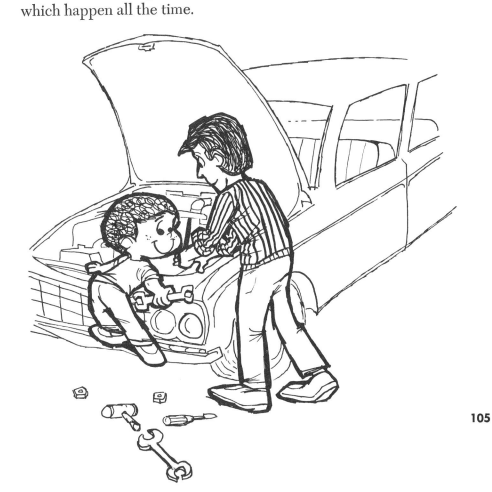

The most important thing these children are not doing with their fathers is talking with them about the matters that can really bring fathers closer to their children. They are not discussing personal things like worries and problems or talking with them truthfully and honestly about what they both think and feel about many subjects. They aren't sharing their hopes, their disappointments, their experiences, and their plans. They are not listening to each other's ideas on subjects such as books, movies, sports, and

world events. Not only can fathers be helpful in answering their children's questions about what they have learned in school, but children these days are learning things their fathers never learned in school, and there's much they can teach their fathers.

Time alone together, when a parent talks with a child in this way, is one of the most enjoyable things you can do with your father. If you have brothers or sisters with whom you must share your father's time, ask him to divide part of the visit so that each of you can spend some time alone with him. Even a few minutes of time alone during each visit can help bring the two of you closer. Many children find that if they discuss some of their problems with their fathers during these periods, many of them can be solved.

Remember, I'm not saying that your father should never take you to fun places. I am saying that other things are more important and do more toward helping you feel better about yourself and the divorce.

DOING ONLY WHAT THE CHILD WANTS, NOT WHAT THE FATHER WANTS Some fathers, because they want to make their children happy, try mainly to do those things which their children want. These are sometimes things which the fathers don't like or may even hate doing. Because of this, the fathers don't have a good time, and they get fussy, and this spoils their visit for the children. What started off as something to make the child happy ends up making him feel sad. It's best to try to do things together which you both enjoy. Then you'll end up having a better time. If your father does things with you that make him miserable, you should talk to him about it and find something you can both enjoy. If you do, you'll have much better times with your father. **107**

This boy liked to watch baseball games. His father hated them, but he took the boy because he thought it would make him happy. By the fifth inning the father was quite cranky, and he barked and snapped at everything the boy did or said. So it ended with the boy's being very sad.

Both of them, however, liked doing shop work. When they did this instead of going to ball games, they both enjoyed being with each other, and they had good times together.

DOING ONLY WHAT THE FATHER WANTS, NOT WHAT THE CHILD WANTS Some fathers do only the things they like, and they do not care whether or not the child wants to do them. Some children with fathers like this say nothing, and so it continues, and they often get to hate their fathers' visits. The children who tell their fathers about this sometimes get them to change their ways.

This girl's father works as a salesman. Every Saturday, and often on Sunday, he took her with him to visit customers. The girl often had to sit alone in the car for a long time, and she was quite bored and unhappy. She began to dread the weekend visits with her father. As long as she said nothing, her father continued to do this

because he didn't realize that his daughter wasn't enjoying herself. The father thought just taking her with him was enough. Although the girl complained a number of times, he still kept taking her. Finally when she told him what was wrong and that she no longer wished to go with him, the father realized he had been making a mistake. They then started to do things together that they both enjoyed.

THE PROBLEM OF HOW MUCH TIME TO SPEND WITH YOUR FATHER In some families there's a rule that the child *must* see his father for one or two days every single week. There may, however, be times when a child doesn't wish to spend time with his father, but prefers to stay home and be alone or play with his friends. Instead, he may be forced to go with his father.

I do not believe a child should be made to see his father more often than he wants to. He should be permitted to choose whether or not he wants to visit on a particular day or weekend. Of course, he must make up his mind in advance so that his father doesn't come for no reason. If you are not being allowed to choose, speak to your parents and tell them your feelings. Some children do not wish to visit and yet do not speak up and tell their parents what they think. Such children often find that if they tell their parents how they truly feel, they will not be forced to visit more often than they wish.

Some parents think that each visit should be for a whole day. They think that since the child does not see his father all week, it is best if they have lots of time together on the weekend. This is true for some but not all families. Sometimes shorter visits are better. Sometimes the father and his child would have a better time if they spent fewer hours together. When they spend too much time together, they often get tired of each other and get on each other's nerves. Sometimes they both wish the visits were shorter, but they do not talk about it with each other. When they do so and then decide to have shorter visits, they are both usually happier when they are together.

Some fathers think that it's important to take all their children with them on visiting day. Sometimes it's better when the children alternate: one time one child goes, another time another child goes. Everyone gets a turn. In this way, the child who goes can spend more time alone with his father. In larger families, a few children can go during one visit and the rest on another visit. Of course, at times it may be more fun for all the children to go together.

Remember, it shouldn't be necessary for you to visit with your father every week if you don't wish to. Also, in some families, everyone is happier when the children alternate their visits: sometimes one child goes, and sometimes another; at times a few may visit, at other times all the children visit together. Lastly, sometimes short visits turn out to be more pleasant than long ones.

BRINGING FRIENDS ALONG WHEN YOU GO OUT WITH YOUR FATHER Many things children like to do are not enjoyable for a grown-up, and many things adults like to do are not fun for children. Because of this, a father may have trouble finding things to do on visiting days which will be enjoyable all day long for both himself and his children. When this happens, fathers and their children get into the kinds of trouble I just told you about, and either the father or the child gets bored or cranky.

One way to make the visits more fun is to bring a friend along. This is especially true for a child who doesn't have a brother or a sister. I am not suggesting that you bring a friend along on every visit, for that would make it hard for your father to do things alone with you. But bringing a friend along once in a while can make the day more enjoyable for both you and your father. You then can have the kinds of fun with your friend that you may not be able to have with your father. Your father may be able to be more relaxed. It is often hard work for a father to keep his children

happy all day long.

Sometimes when a father brings his child's friend along, he will do little or nothing with his child but will just let the kids play together the entire time. If your father does this and you are lonely for him, tell him how you feel so that you'll be able to spend more time alone with him.

Remember, having a friend come along once in a while can be a good thing, and it can *add to the pleasure of the visit*. But friends should not come too often or you will have little time to spend alone with your father.

ACTING TOO GROWN-UP WITH YOUR FATHER In the last chapter, I told you that some boys try to act like husbands to their mothers. There are also some girls who try to act like wives to their fathers. Such a girl might cook for him, talk to him like a grown-up, put on makeup when he visits, and want to go many places alone with him. Some fathers like their daughters to behave this way. Generally, if a girl and her father do these things too much, she will have problems later when she wants to date and marry. It is, therefore, a bad idea. Also, such girls often have trouble with their girl friends, who usually do not like a child who acts so much like an adult.

ACTING LIKE A BABY WITH YOUR FATHER In the last chapter, I also told you about boys and girls who act like babies with their mothers. These children try to get their fathers to baby them as well, or their fathers might even enjoy babying them. This is a bad idea. It might be nice for these children to get extra attention and care, but they will have trouble getting along with children their own age, who will call them "baby" and tease them because they don't act their age. Later on, such children often have trouble   **113**

dating, marrying, and making friends. A good father will not baby his children.

WHEN YOUR FATHER TALKS ABOUT YOUR MOTHER In the last chapter, I told you that some mothers are not to be trusted when they talk about their child's father. There are also some fathers who are not to be trusted when they talk about their child's mother. Such fathers say very bad things about the mother which are not true. They may even say that the mother hates her own child when she doesn't.

If your father is like this, it's best not to take what he says about your mother too seriously unless you are very sure that he's right. Often he can't be completely trusted when he says bad things about your mother, but he can usually be believed when he speaks about other things.

FATHERS WHO DO NOT VISIT Next I will talk about fathers who live close by but do not visit, and fathers who live far away and hardly ever call or write. Fortunately, there are very few such fathers.

It's sad to say, but these fathers either do not love their children at all, or they love them very little. As you grow older you'll learn that no one is perfect; everyone has his faults, and this is true of your parents as well. The fathers I am talking about may be all right in many ways, but they have a terrible problem in that they are not able to love their own children.

If your father is like this, it does not mean that you are no good or that no one can love you. Because your father doesn't love you, it doesn't mean that you're not lovable. Something is very wrong

with a parent who can't love his own child. This is sad for him because he's missing out on one of the greatest joys in life. There's an old saying, "He's more to be pitied than scorned." This means that the more pity and the less anger you feel toward such a father, the better off you'll be.

The father of a girl I know did not show much interest in her, and he hardly ever came to visit. One day when talking about her father, she said, "Poor damn Dad!" This was a good way to show that she had pity for him and, at the same time, to let out some of her anger.

Some children with fathers like this keep wishing and hoping that they'll change, and they try many things to get their fathers to love them. If you do this and he still doesn't show interest after a few times, it's best to try to forget him and to try getting fun from friendships with others, both young and old.

There's another old saying, "Don't beat a dead horse." A slow horse might go faster when he is hit softly with a stick, but a dead horse will never move, no matter how long he is beaten. This saying means that one should not waste one's time trying to beat the horse into moving, for he won't. In the same way, if your father shows over and over again that he doesn't love you, stop trying to get him to change. Don't beat a dead horse!

Some children whose fathers never, or hardly ever, visit will deny that anything is wrong with him and act at times as if he were perfect. Nothing anyone tells them about their father's faults is believed. They keep insisting that their father is perfect, and they make up all kinds of silly excuses to explain why he never, or hardly ever, visits. Refusing to face the facts only makes it harder for these children to handle the problems of divorce, and this usually just adds to their troubles.

What can you do then if you hardly ever see your father? The most important thing you can do is to form good friendships with children your own age and with men who can be part-time, substitute fathers. There are many clubs where children who live with only one parent can find such substitutes. In such clubs, adults and children go on outings and picnics, play games, visit interesting places, and do most of the things that children normally do with their fathers. If your mother does not belong to such a club, ask her to join one; they are to be found in most cities and towns. Also, scoutmasters, coaches, counselors, and group leaders can be good father-substitutes. They can be met in schools, churches, playgrounds, and youth centers everywhere. If you have not joined such a group, now is the time to do so.

8.

HOW TO GET ALONG BETTER WITH PARENTS WHO ARE LIVING APART

SPECIAL PROBLEMS arise when a child spends part of his time with one parent and part with the other. Most often these problems come about because the parents, although divorced, are still fighting. They haven't yet settled all their differences and they cannot fight so easily because they're living apart. Each one tries to use the child to help him in his fight against the other. It would be far better for the child if they were to stop, for then he would not have many of the problems I am going to discuss now.

USING YOU AS A SPY OR TATTLETALE Some parents try to use their child as a spy. Each parent asks him many questions about the other, such as whether the other one is dating or spending a lot of money. The child, because he wants to please, may try to answer these questions. This is a big mistake. He should tell his parents that he will not be a tattletale. One reason for doing this is that he is only helping the fighting to continue by being a spy. If he were to stop giving information, his parents might fight less. Also, no one really likes a spy, including the spy himself. **117**

Your parents may say they like you more because you give them information, but deep inside, they like you less for doing so. If your mother knows that you'll tell your father personal things about her, she'll not trust you, and your father will not trust you if you tell your mother about his personal life. Also, you cannot feel good about yourself if you're a tattletale.

Now, I am not telling you that you should say nothing to either parent about your visits with the other. You will learn there are certain things it is best not to talk about. It's hard at first to figure out exactly what these things are, but most children do learn them. If the question has little to do with you—for instance, if it's about the private life of your parent—it's probably best not to answer it. It's best to answer such a question by saying, "Please stop trying to turn me into a tattletale." If certain topics seem to lead to more fighting between your parents, it's best not to answer questions about them. Two subjects which parents often want information about are whether the other is dating and what kind of things the other parent spends money on. There are also other things which cause fights, and you have to learn which ones apply in your family.

THE TUG OF WAR   Sometimes a mother tries to get the child to side with her against the father, or a father tries to get the child to side with him against the mother. Each parent wants the child to agree that the other parent is wrong. When both parents try to do this, the child is caught in the middle. If he takes his mother's side, his father may get angry with him. If he takes his father's side, his mother may get angry with him. What can you do if you are in such a situation?

One thing you can do is to refuse to take sides or get involved in the battle. Do not join with one parent in his plots against the

other. Do not carry messages that have to do with their fighting.

If this is happening to you, another thing you can do is be very careful about what you believe when one parent tells you bad things about the other. Although your parents may try to be very honest and truthful with you, it's hard for them to be truthful about each other even to themselves. They cannot be completely trusted in the things they say about each other, especially the bad things. You have to be very careful to believe only those things you are very sure of or that you actually see yourself.

It's important to remember that people are not perfect; they have good and bad sides; they are right in certain things and wrong in others. Most often, both parents are wrong in some arguments and right in others. It's unusual for the mother or the father to be right all the time. Sometimes your mother will be right, other times your father will be. Sometimes you will not be able to decide which one is right. When you listen to your mother, she will sound right. When you listen to your father, he will sound right. At times, even psychiatrists have trouble figuring out who is right.

The best thing you can do when one or both of your parents tries to get you to side with him against the other is refuse to join

the battle and be very careful not to believe every bad thing one of them says about the other. You can, however, usually believe other things they may talk about, things which have nothing to do with the divorce.

PLAYING ONE PARENT AGAINST THE OTHER Some children try to get each of their parents to like them more by saying the bad things that they know the parent they're with would like to hear about the other. For instance, when he's with his mother, the child will tell her bad things about his father and when he's with his father, he will tell him bad things about the mother. Some children just tell the bad and not the good things, others make up things. Doing this is called "playing one parent against the other." Each of his parents may like hearing such tales. However, the child knows he is tricking his parents and being false to them, so when he does this, he feels bad about himself. And, sooner or later, his parents will learn what is going on, and then they will distrust the child and like him less.

When divorced parents are spiteful to one another, the child may use the situation to get things he may want from them which he does not really need. For instance, this girl kept telling her father that her mother always said that he was cheap with his

money and that he never bought presents for his children. Her father believed her story, and he started to buy presents for the girl even though she didn't really need them. When she was with her mother, she told her that the father kept saying that the

mother went around with too many men and didn't spend enough time at home. The mother believed this lie, and she started to date less and spend more time with the girl than she really needed to.

Although this girl got more presents from her father and spent more time with her mother, she felt very bad about being such a liar. And when her parents finally found out what was going on,

they distrusted her for a long time, even after she had stopped lying. So you can see from this that the liar usually ends up fooling himself much more than he fools the people to whom he lies.

USING YOU AS A TOOL OR WEAPON Parents who are still fighting after the divorce will at times try to hurt or control one another by doing something to the child. This is called "using the child as a tool or weapon." For example, the mother may not let the child visit his father because the father does things she doesn't like. She may tell the father that when he changes his ways, she'll let the children visit. Or the father may not send money for the care of the children because the mother is doing things he doesn't approve of. He may tell her that he'll only send money if she behaves the way he wants her to.

Such a situation is very bad, and often there's little a child can do here but accept it. There are a few things he can try, however. He can tell each of his parents that they are making him suffer for things which have nothing to do with him and that this is not only unfair but also very cruel of them. He can tell his parents that their behavior only causes him to have less love and respect for them, for how can they expect him to love and respect them if they hurt him for something he had nothing to do with. Sometimes telling this to parents is helpful.

If your mother won't let you see your father, remember that she will not have control when you are older. Then you can see him as much as the two of you wish. If your father doesn't send the money he should, you'll not starve or be without clothing or a home. Even if your mother has no money at all, cities and towns usually have money to give to mothers when things like this happen. **125**

However, a child often may not be able to do anything about such situations. He should remember that the time will come when he'll be grown, and then he'll not be so helpless, and he'll not be hurt so easily by other people's problems.

If your parents do the things I discussed in this chapter, you should get along with them better if you follow the suggestions I've given you.

9.

HOW TO GET ALONG BETTER WITH YOUR STEPFATHER AND STEPMOTHER

IF YOUR DIVORCED mother marries again, her new husband will be called your "stepfather." If your divorced father marries again, his new wife will be called your "stepmother." It's often a very good thing for parents to marry again, for the home is then complete with a father and mother, and usually both the parents and the children are happier. Sometimes a stepmother or stepfather is nicer to a child than his real mother or father was. Then, of course, the child is much happier.

First, I'll talk about stepfathers, then about stepmothers.

ABOUT STEPFATHERS Many children talk a lot about wanting their divorced mothers to marry again so they'll have a new father. However, many children get frightened or angry when a new man **127**

appears and it looks as if he's going to marry their mother. These children may then change their minds and tell their mothers that they don't want her to get married.

One reason for this is that new things are often frightening—even for grown-ups. When a mother gets married again, the child does not know what to expect. He may not know what kind of person his new father will be, and he may think that the worst rather than the best things will happen. These fears most often go away after the child gets to know the stepfather better and sees what he's really like.

Sometimes the new stepfather wants very much for you to like him, and he may soon show this by hugging you a lot, buying you too many presents, and trying to be with you too much. If so, he does not realize that true friendship and love grow slowly, not quickly. He wants to be your friend right away and doesn't realize that the best way to become your friend is the slow and natural way. Don't let this scare you away or cause you not to like him. He probably likes you and is showing it in a mistaken way.

Often children fear their new stepfather because they do not trust men. Because their first father left home, they are afraid that all men will leave. They're afraid to like him too much for fear of being disappointed again. This is a common belief, and your mother probably had the same thoughts about him. However, just because one man has left, it does not mean that another one will leave. Your mother is probably trying harder this time to make sure that he's the right man for her so that this marriage won't break up too.

Some children change their mind about their mother marrying again when they see that the new father would take away some of the time they once had with their mother. Often they get angry about this and try to tell the man to go away, and they try to get their mother not to marry him. This dislike may grow when they see him hug and kiss their mother, be with her a lot around the house, and go off with her on evening dates or for even longer sometimes. They wish they could go back to the time when they had their mother all to themselves. It also hurts them to see how much their mother enjoys being with this new man, and they think that she cannot really love them if she loves him so much.

First, it's important to remember that love isn't like a piece of pie with only so much for each person, and that if you give more to one, the other person gets less. Love is more like a spring of water. A person can give large amounts of it to a number of people. Because your mother loves this new man and spends a lot of time with him, this does not mean she loves you less. Second, it's important to realize that the happier your mother is, the better mother she'll be to you. If this new man makes her a happier person, you'll see that she'll be a better mother to you, will be more patient with you, and will enjoy her time with you even more. That's one of the nice things about love—loving the new man makes her enjoy all the things she does much more, and this will make her love you more because she'll enjoy you more. Lastly, it's important to remember that as you grow older you'll have more and more chances to make friends of your own with whom you can have all the fun your mother is having. Someday, you too will marry a person you can have all to yourself and with whom you can do many wonderful things.

Some children have trouble with their real fathers and take it out on their stepfathers. They may be very angry at their fathers

but hold in their anger. When this happens, the anger builds up inside the child; he becomes cranky and fussy, and then he lets out his anger on someone else—like his stepfather. He may then see his stepfather as being mean or cruel when he really isn't. When such a child speaks to his real father about the things which

bother him and then settles these problems with his real father, he has less trouble with his stepfather.

Sometimes there's a problem over what to call one's stepfather. Most children don't want to use the same name for their stepfather and their father. They consider their real father someone special, and it therefore makes them feel uncomfortable to call someone else by the same name. What should the child do in this case? The first thing to remember in answering this question is that you should not use any name you are not comfortable with. Don't let yourself be made to use a name you don't wish to. Generally, there are a number of names which children use: Father, Dad, Pop, and Pa are the most common. Some children will use one of these for their real father and another for their stepfather. Others may call their stepfather by his first name, if he agrees to this. Some make up a special name all their own for their step-father. Such a name might be a combination of the word Father, Dad, Pop, or Pa and the stepfather's first name. Again, it's important to use only a name that is natural for you and not one you are being forced to use.

Some children are very disappointed in their new stepfather. One reason for this is that he may not love them as much as they had hoped. It's important to realize that your stepfather married your mother because he loved her, not you. If he comes to love you, that's fine, so much the better. But you aren't his real child. Although some men love their stepchildren as their very own, others do not. If your stepfather doesn't love you, it doesn't mean you're not worth loving. It just means that he doesn't love you. You'll continue to be disappointed as long as you continue to hope that he'll love you when he cannot or won't.

Another reason some children are disappointed in their step-father is that they had hoped for a person who was perfect or almost perfect. Although such children have real fathers who often have many faults, they hope their stepfather will have none. No one is perfect. Everyone has faults. These children will continue to be disappointed as long as they keep wishing that their step-father be perfect.

Many children hope that their divorced parents will get married to one another again. Although their parents keep telling them that this won't happen, they still keep hoping. When one of the parents then marries someone else, it's hard for the child to keep on wishing that his original parents would marry again. This is good because it helps the child stop wasting his time by hoping for

132 something that cannot happen.

ABOUT STEPMOTHERS Now many of the things I've said about stepfathers are true of stepmothers as well. Most children whose parents are divorced live with their mother. If she gets married again, they live with their stepfather as well, and the stepfather then becomes important to them. Most children of divorced parents don't live with their father. If their father gets married again, they have a stepmother. Usually children do not see a stepmother as often as they do a stepfather; therefore, she is not so important to them.

A father sometimes spends less time with his children after he marries again. His new wife wants him to spend time with her, and often she will not like it when he goes off with you. If you get along well with your stepmother, you'll probably see more of your father. Remember well what I have just said because if you do, it can make a big difference in how often you see your father and what kinds of times you'll have when you're with him. In addition, your stepmother is a person who will possibly become very friendly with you and help you not to be sad and lonely.

Some children have troubles with their mother and take it out on their stepmother. They may be afraid to tell their real mother what is bothering them, and so they hold it in. This makes them fussy, and then they let their anger out on their stepmother. They may then come to look upon their stepmothers as being bad or evil when they really aren't. Such a child will get along better with his stepmother when he settles his problems with his real mother. As I have told you many times before, the purpose of anger is to help you when you have trouble with someone. Talk to that person about it; don't hold the anger in. Let the anger help you solve the problem. One thing that may happen if you hold your anger in is that you'll let it out on the wrong person. Taking it out on your stepmother is an example of this.

Some children have a problem over what to call their step-mother. Since the child already has one real mother, he doesn't feel comfortable using the same name for his stepmother. He considers his mother someone very special, and he doesn't feel right when he calls someone else by the same name. What should a child do then? The important thing to remember is to use only a name that you are comfortable with. Don't let yourself be forced into using a name that you don't wish to use. Some children feel comfortable when they call one person "Mother" and the other person "Mom." Most do not like to use exactly the same name for both. Others will call their stepmother by her first name, when she agrees to this. Some prefer to make up a special name for their stepmother. Such a name could be some combination of the word Mother, Mom, or Ma and the stepmother's first name. The important thing to remember is that whatever name you use it should be one you feel comfortable with. It should not be one that is

134 forced on you.

Although new problems may arise when parents get married again, children are usually happier and better off in a complete home, one with both a mother and a father—even if one of the parents is a stepparent.

10.

OTHER PROBLEMS CHILDREN OF DIVORCED PARENTS HAVE

PROBLEMS WITH OTHER CHILDREN Some children of divorced parents have problems with children whose parents are not divorced. These children can sometimes be very cruel, and they may make fun of children from divorced homes. They may think that you're different or strange in some way, and their parents may not want them to play with you.

Why does this happen?

One of the reasons is that many adults have strange ideas about divorce. They may think that people who get divorced are bad, sinful, or strange. They don't realize that divorce is a very sad thing and that it's most often caused by mistakes people make or problems they cannot control. Instead of feeling sorry for and trying to help divorced people, they may laugh at them, hate them, keep themselves separate from them, or act strangely toward them in other ways. They may teach these odd ideas to their children, who then begin to think that the children of divorced parents are bad, sinful, or strange.

Another reason some children are cruel is that they feel bad **137** themselves, and they try to feel better by making fun of others. They pick especially on those who have a weakness or those who have had something sad happen to them. They try to make themselves feel bigger and better by trying to make others feel smaller. This never works. No matter how much they pick on others or laugh at them, it doesn't help them feel better about themselves.

What can you do if this happens to you?

Some children try to hide the fact that their parents are divorced. They may make up all kinds of stories to explain why their father is not at home. They may not allow children to visit their home because they're afraid that others might see that their father is not living there. They may even stop playing with children from fear that others will learn their secret.

This is one of the worst things a child can do, because a person who does this only feels worse about himself. He knows that he's lying, and this makes him feel bad about himself. He always fears that others will learn his secret. Being afraid all the time that others will learn about the divorce is far worse than anything that could possibly have happened if they had found out in the first place. And if other children do find out later, they will have a hard time trusting a child who lied in this way. Lastly, the child who stays away from others because he doesn't want them to learn of the divorce leads a very lonely life.

So what can you do if people are cruel to you or make fun of you because your parents are divorced?

First, it's important to remember that just because other people think you're bad, sinful, or strange, it does not mean that you are. You are what you are, not necessarily what people say you are. Sometimes, of course, what people say about you is right, but
138 sometimes what they say about you is not. Some people think that

everything others say about them has to be true. Sometimes it is, and sometimes it isn't. You have to decide for yourself whether what others say is right or wrong.

If someone were to say that your hair was purple and your skin green, this would not make your hair purple and your skin green. You could look at yourself in the mirror and see that it wasn't so. Then you would see that something must be wrong with a person who could say such a foolish thing.

If someone said that your hair was brown and your eyes were blue, and you looked in the mirror and saw this was so, you would know the person was right and you would agree with him.

Remember too the old saying, "Sticks and stones may break my
bones, but names will never harm me." No matter what other

children *say* about you, it cannot really hurt you. This saying is a
good answer to children who make fun of you for any reason.

In the same way, when children call you names or think that you're sinful and strange because your parents are divorced, this doesn't make it true. You know that you aren't, and so you know something must be wrong with what they've said. If you'll remember this, it may help you feel better about yourself.

It's also important to remember that children who make fun of you because they feel bad about themselves are only trying to make themselves feel bigger by trying to make you feel smaller. When you understand this, you may not be as bothered by what they say.

The best thing you can do with people who have foolish ideas about divorce is be your natural, true, honest self and go about doing everything just as you would if your parents were not divorced. The fact that your parents are divorced has nothing to do with most of the things you do with other children at school and at play. If you're your natural self, most children will behave toward you as they would if your parents were not divorced. The main thing that other children care about is whether you're nice and how much fun it is to be with you. If you play well with them

and are friendly, most children will want to play with you even though your parents are divorced. Even if they call you names once in a while or have the same strange ideas their parents have about divorce, they'll like you and want to be with you if you are a likable person.

CHILDREN WHO FEEL BAD ABOUT THEMSELVES Some children are never laughed at by others or told that they are strange or bad because their parents are divorced, and yet they feel this way anyway. They think they aren't as good as children whose parents are happily married. I think it's just that they are not as lucky. Through no fault of their own, some children are born to parents who get divorced. This doesn't make these children bad or strange or less lovable; they're just less lucky.

Remember too that many children whose parents are living together are no happier or luckier than you. Many parents stay married even though they're very unhappy together. They stay together because they think that their children are better off this way. As I mentioned earlier, psychiatrists know that this often is

not so and that the children would often be better off if they did get divorced. These children may suffer from problems that are even greater than yours. You're certainly luckier than they are. Don't think that every child whose parents are still married is better off than you are. Many of them are much worse off.

Many children whose parents are divorced feel bad about themselves because most, if not all, of the children around them have parents who are still married. They feel they are different, and they think that there are very few children like themselves. When other children talk about doing things with both of their parents, they are sad to think that they cannot do such things too.

These children often feel better when their parents join special clubs for divorced people. There they can be with many other children whose situation is similar to theirs. Then they can see that they aren't the only ones with problems, and they feel less different than others and better about themselves. Also, the children in these clubs can learn from one another some better ways of dealing with the problems that children of divorced parents have. There are millions of children whose parents are divorced, and such children are to be found in almost every city, town, and village. The number grows each year, and clubs for them are being started all the time. Ask your mother and father if it's possible for you to join such a club. If you can, you'll have a good chance of feeling better about your troubles.

CHILDREN WHO ARE ASHAMED OF THEMSELVES BECAUSE OF THEIR PARENTS' BEHAVIOR Many divorces come about because one or both parents have very serious problems. A father may drink too much. Another father may gamble away most of his **144** earnings, and as a result there is not enough money for the family.

Some fathers do such bad things that they are sent to jail. Some fathers spend a lot of time with other women, and this is usually quite painful to their wives and children. There are also mothers who behave badly. They may go out with other men, or they may rarely clean the home or cook a good full meal for their families. Sometimes parents fight and scream so much that the police have to be called to quiet them. Some parents behave strangely and have to go to a special kind of hospital, called a mental hospital. Such hospitals are for people whose problems and troubles are very great. These are just a few of the terrible things that can happen to parents—things that may have caused the divorce.

Many of the children whose parents do some of the things I have just mentioned are very ashamed of themselves because of their parents' behavior. They think they are no good because people find fault with their parents. This is a wrong way of thinking. It is sad for a child when he has a parent who does such things, but it does not mean that the child of such parents is any less worthy a person. He's just had the bad luck to have such a parent. If you think that you are less acceptable because you have such a parent, you are not thinking correctly.

YOUR EXTRA JOBS AND RESPONSIBILITIES Children of divorced parents have more to do on their own than children whose parents are married. They have to do more jobs around the house, help more in caring for their younger brothers and sisters, and do many more grown-up things. These added responsibilities, if there are not too many of them, can be healthy and good for a child. They will help him grow up, and he will learn many things which will be helpful to him when he's older. This is one of the few ways in which children of divorced parents may be better off than children **145**

whose parents are happily married.

Most children take on the extra jobs willingly. However, a few refuse to do them and try instead to go back to the time when they were babies, when everything was done for them and given to them. Often such children have mothers who help this happen by babying them. Such children and their mothers are making a very big mistake because these children will not learn how to do many of the things all older children and grown-ups have to do if they are to get along in the world. When they grow up, these children may be afraid to take jobs or to get married and take care of children of their own.

Some children use the divorce to excuse themselves from taking on their usual responsibilities. They think that just because their **146** parents are divorced they should be pitied and that they should be given special privileges. They then try to avoid doing the things they should. They may take the attitude that people should not expect them to do the things other children are expected to do—like chores, errands, unpleasant jobs, and homework—just because their parents are divorced.

Any adult who goes along with these children in their avoidance of their responsibilities is making a great mistake indeed, for he is not helping them grow up, but is instead helping them remain babies. Other children will look upon such babied children as "privileged characters" and will not want to be friends with them.

Children of married parents have two grown-ups living in the home who usually give them love and friendship. Children of divorced parents have only one. Such children have to make up for the loss by finding substitutes elsewhere. They have to make it their business to find friends so that they'll be less lonely. Few children get friends by just sitting around and doing nothing. They have to go out where the children are and mix with them. They have to invite other children to their houses and accept invitations from them to theirs.

They have to join the clubs where children are—clubs at school and churches and Y's—clubs like the Scouts, Little League, and the many others which are to be found in almost every city and town. These clubs are helpful in many ways. When he's with other children, a child feels less lonely, and he can enjoy many friendships. Also, the counselors or leaders of these clubs often help a child make up for the loss he feels because of the absence of his father. Many of the things you might do with a father can be done with club leaders. Even the saddest and loneliest children feel better when they make more friends, both young and old.

As you grow older, it'll be easier for you to get together with **147**

children because you'll be able to do more on your own. Teen-agers have clubs and groups of their own and go out on dates, and in this way they meet more people with whom they can have good times. Of course, when you are even older, be it at college or at work or whatever else you do, there will always be people you can like and love, people who'll like and love you as well.

What I have just said is very important because many children

from divorced homes do not wish to grow up and marry. Just

because their parents' marriage was a bad one, they think that all marriages are bad and full of arguments and sadness. They may even have been told this by their parents. This is not so. Many people are quite happy in their marriage. This doesn't mean that there's never any unhappiness or battling in a good marriage. All marriages have some. But in good, happy marriages, there's not too much. Just because your parents were divorced because there was so much fighting and sadness in their marriage doesn't mean you cannot someday have a good marriage of your own.

11.

IF YOU HAVE TO SEE A THERAPIST

SOME CHILDREN of divorced parents have so many troubles that they need a special kind of helper called a "therapist." I'm a child psychiatrist, and I'm one kind of therapist. There are many other types as well. Usually divorce alone doesn't cause a child so much difficulty that he has to see a therapist. If his troubles are that great, it means he has other problems as well, which have little or nothing to do with the divorce.

THE KINDS OF PEOPLE THERAPISTS SEE   Some children think that only "crazy" people have to go to psychiatrists or other types of therapists. If such children then have to see one themselves, they're very ashamed of it, and they feel very bad about themselves and think that something terrible must be wrong with them. Most children who see therapists don't look or behave any differently than other people. They're children who have special problems in a few parts of their lives but who do quite well in most things. Not everything is wrong with them, just a few things.   **151**

CHILDREN WHO ARE ASHAMED TO SEE A THERAPIST   Some children who think that it's a terrible and shameful thing to see a therapist refuse to go. This is a bad mistake because they then continue to have problems. If they had gone to a therapist, they might have cleared up many of them.

Others go even though they are ashamed, but they're very careful never to let anyone know they do. They try to keep the whole thing a big secret. They think that if anyone learned of it, he wouldn't want to have anything to do with them any more. Such children don't realize that their problems are only one small part of themselves and that the rest is often quite good and healthy. They also don't know that the main thing that other children are interested in is whether you are friendly and fun to be with. If you are, they'll want to be with you even if you do go to a therapist.

There may be some parents in your neighborhood who have strange ideas about people who go to therapists. They may think that the children who do go are crazy and that terrible things will happen to their own children if they play with a child who goes to a therapist. These people are often the same ones who are foolish enough to think that something must be terribly wrong with someone whose parents are divorced. If you're going to a therapist, don't take these people seriously. Remember, there's probably much more wrong with them than with you since they think the way they do. But, most important, their children will want to be with you if you're friendly and fun to be with—even though you are seeing a therapist.

WHAT THERAPISTS DO   Let me tell you a little about what therapists do. Although some are doctors, they do not usually give examinations or shots. At times they give pills to help children become less nervous, jumpy, and fussy. At the therapist's office, children usually draw pictures, play with dolls, puppets, and other games, and tell stories. Therapists like to hear about dreams, for dreams tell them something about the problems that are deep inside you, which you may not know too much about. Therapists also talk with children and parents about many of the problems I have discussed in this book. All of these things can help a child worry less and feel better about his troubles.   **153**

Although most children of divorced parents don't have to go to therapists, they all could feel somewhat better about their problems if they talked to their parents and asked them questions. If you're not going to a therapist, I'm sure you will feel better about some of your troubles if you talk them over with your parents.

12.

FIELDS' RULE

IN THE EARLY DAYS of the movies, there was a very famous actor named W. C. Fields. He was a comedian, and he appeared in many funny movies, some of which are still shown today. Many of the funny things he said were also very wise. Some of these are still repeated today, and they have become almost like old sayings. One of these was:

If at first you don't succeed . . .

try, try again. . . .

If after that, you still don't succeed . . .

forget it. . . .

Don't make a big fool of yourself!

This is such a wise saying that I call it Fields' Rule, and I often tell it to patients of mine, both young and old. Many people refuse to learn from their mistakes, and they keep trying to succeed in a thing when they should have realized long ago that they could not.

Many children of divorced parents would not have some of the problems they do if they followed Fields' Rule. Many children keep trying to get their parents to marry one another again when they will not. Others keep trying to get a parent to love them when he cannot. They often become stubborn about these things, will not give up hope, will not admit that it cannot be done, and will not forget it. They will not try to do the things which might help solve their problems.

So always remember Fields' Rule!

I've told you many things about divorce. It's hard to understand all of these things at once. Read again those parts you do not understand and ask your parents about them. It is often most helpful to discuss these things with them.

Remember, if you're worried about something, talk to your parents about your worries and ask them questions. If you do this, I'm sure you'll feel better about your problems.

EPILOGUE

I WROTE THIS BOOK because I wished that the children of divorced parents would read it and that they would then feel better about their troubles. I hope that my wish has come true.

Clubs for divorced parents 144